Chocolate Brownie Tea Kettle

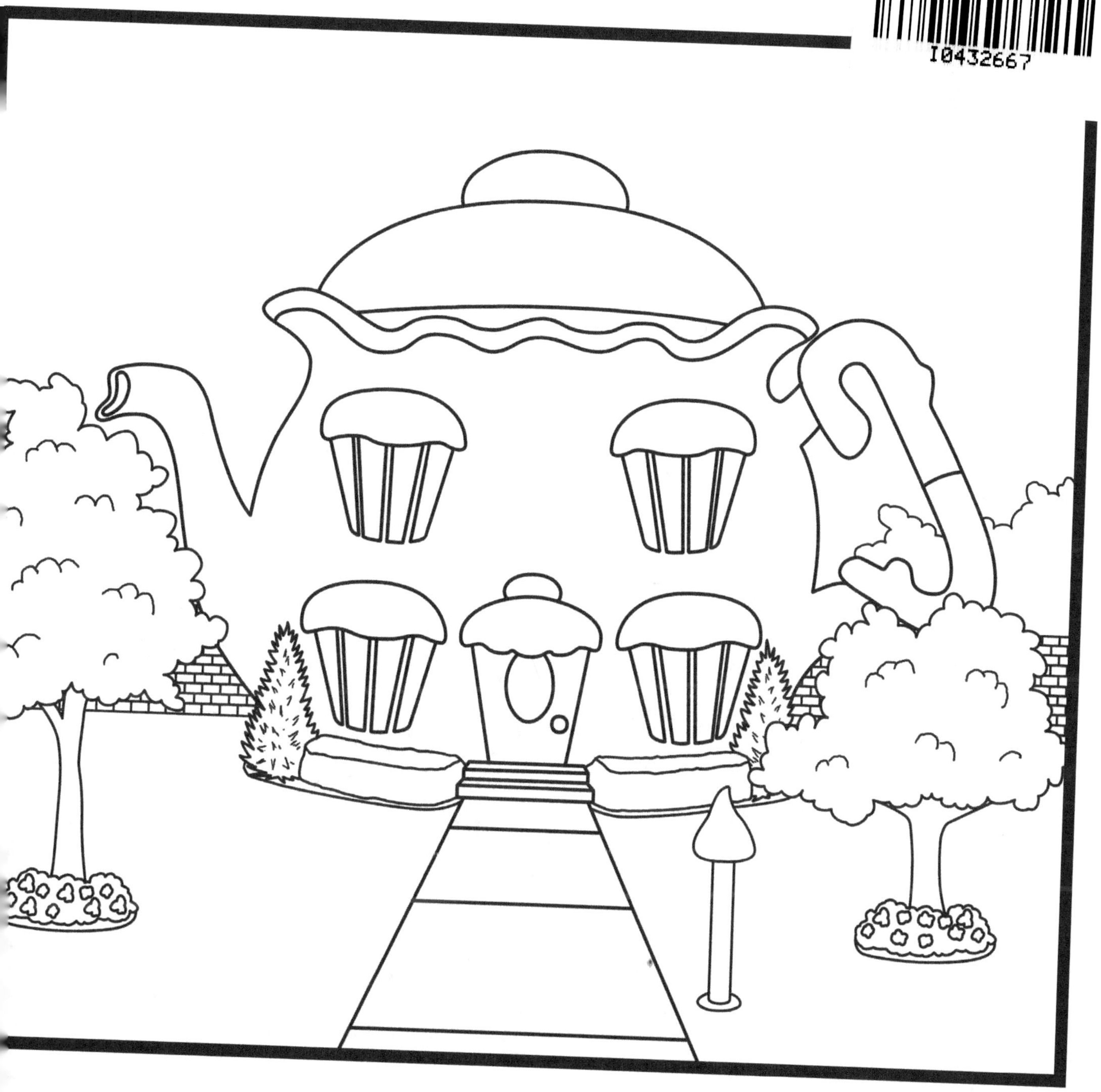

Banana Pudding Tea Kettle

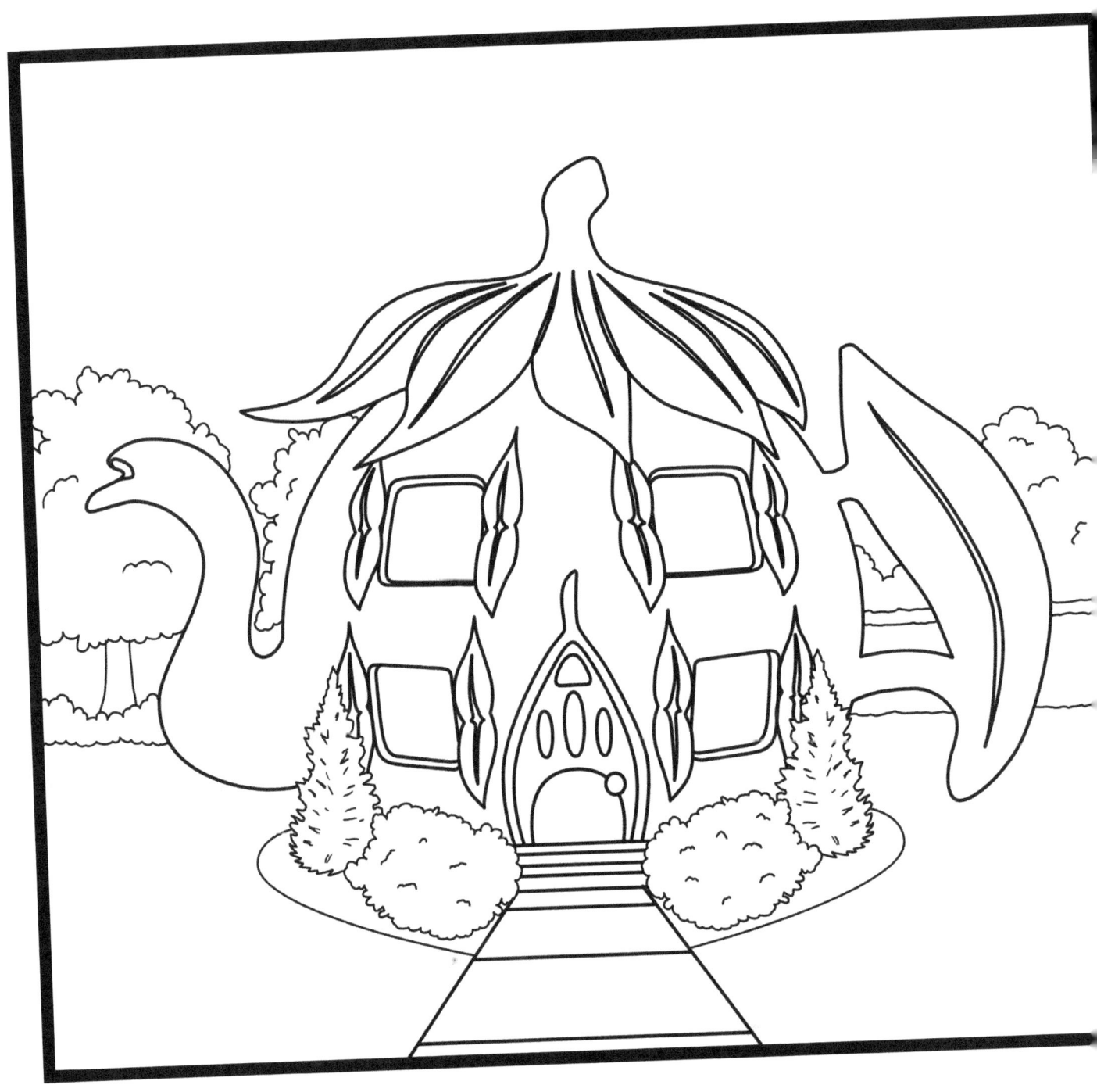

Berry Library Tea Kettle

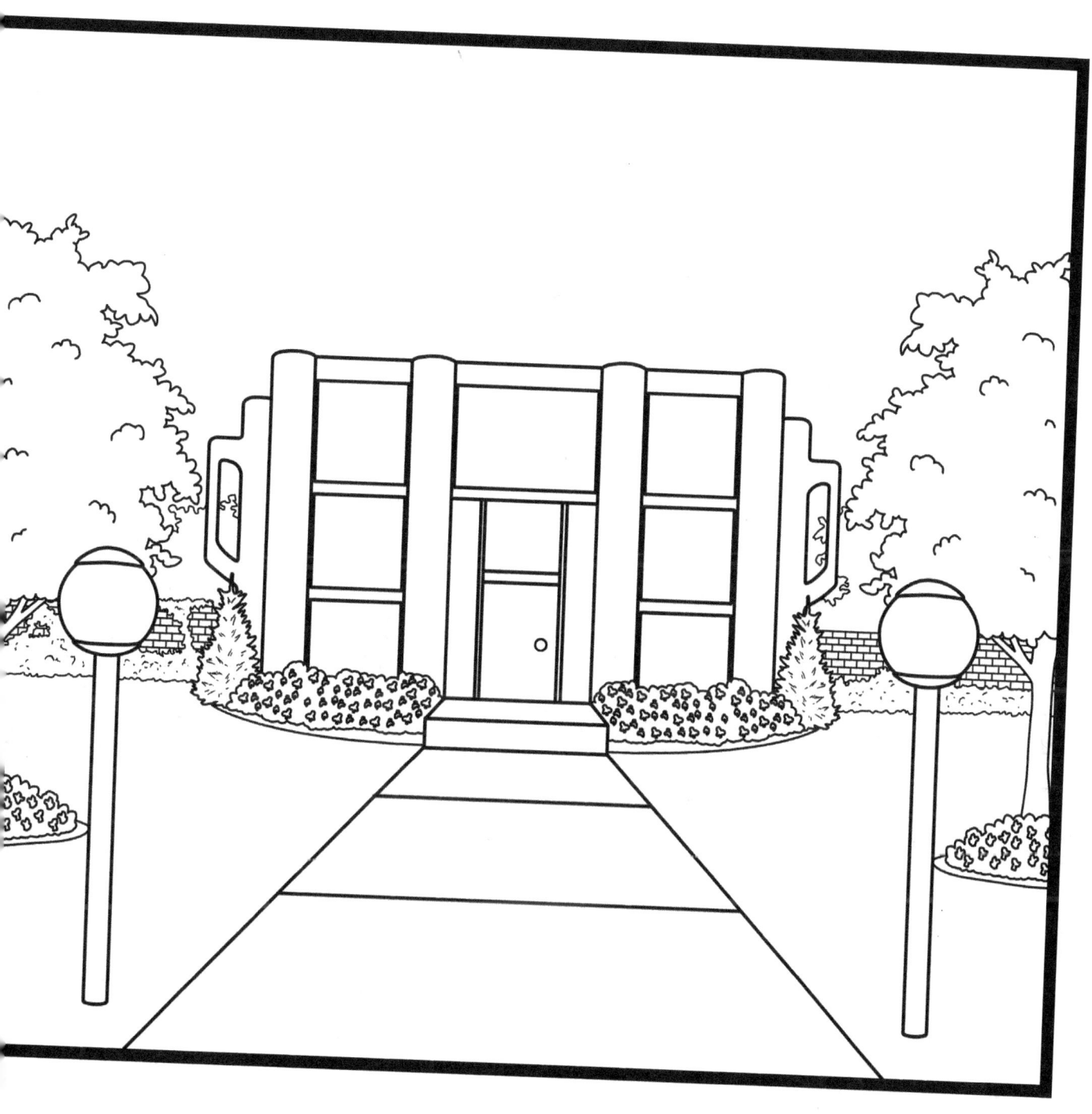

Blushful Pinkness Tea Kettle

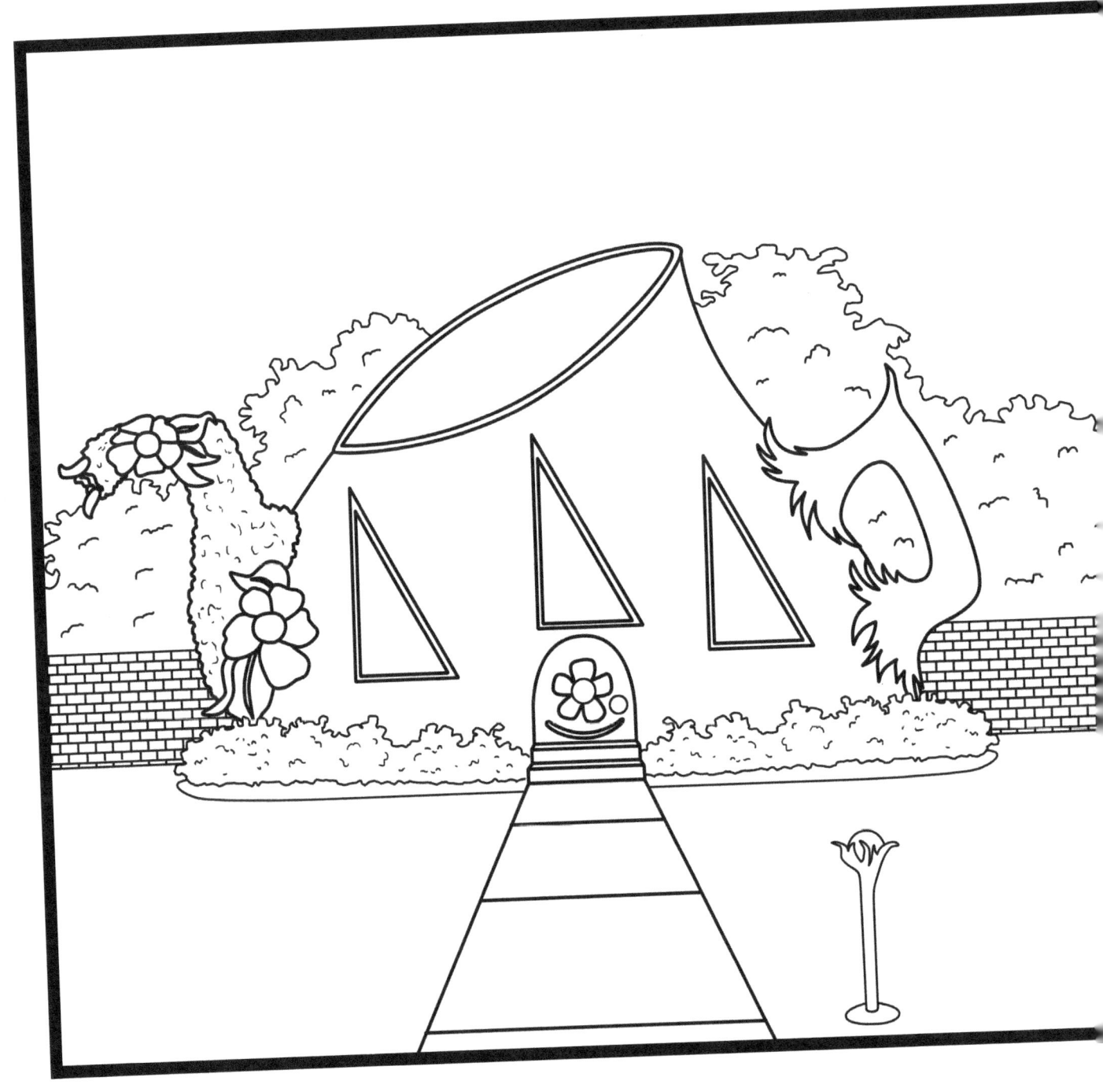

Myra Flower House Tea Kettle

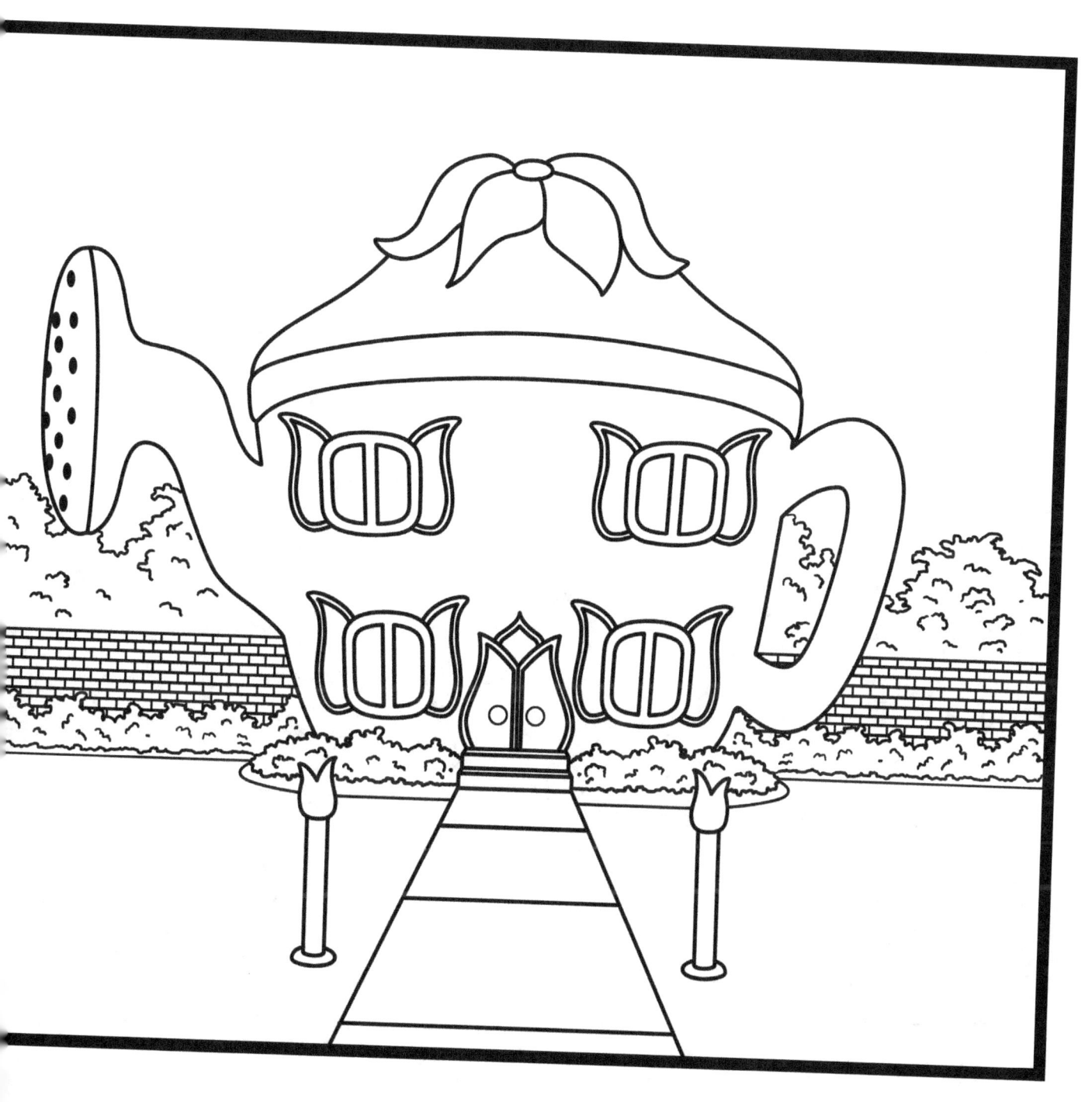

Peachy Puff Tea Kettle

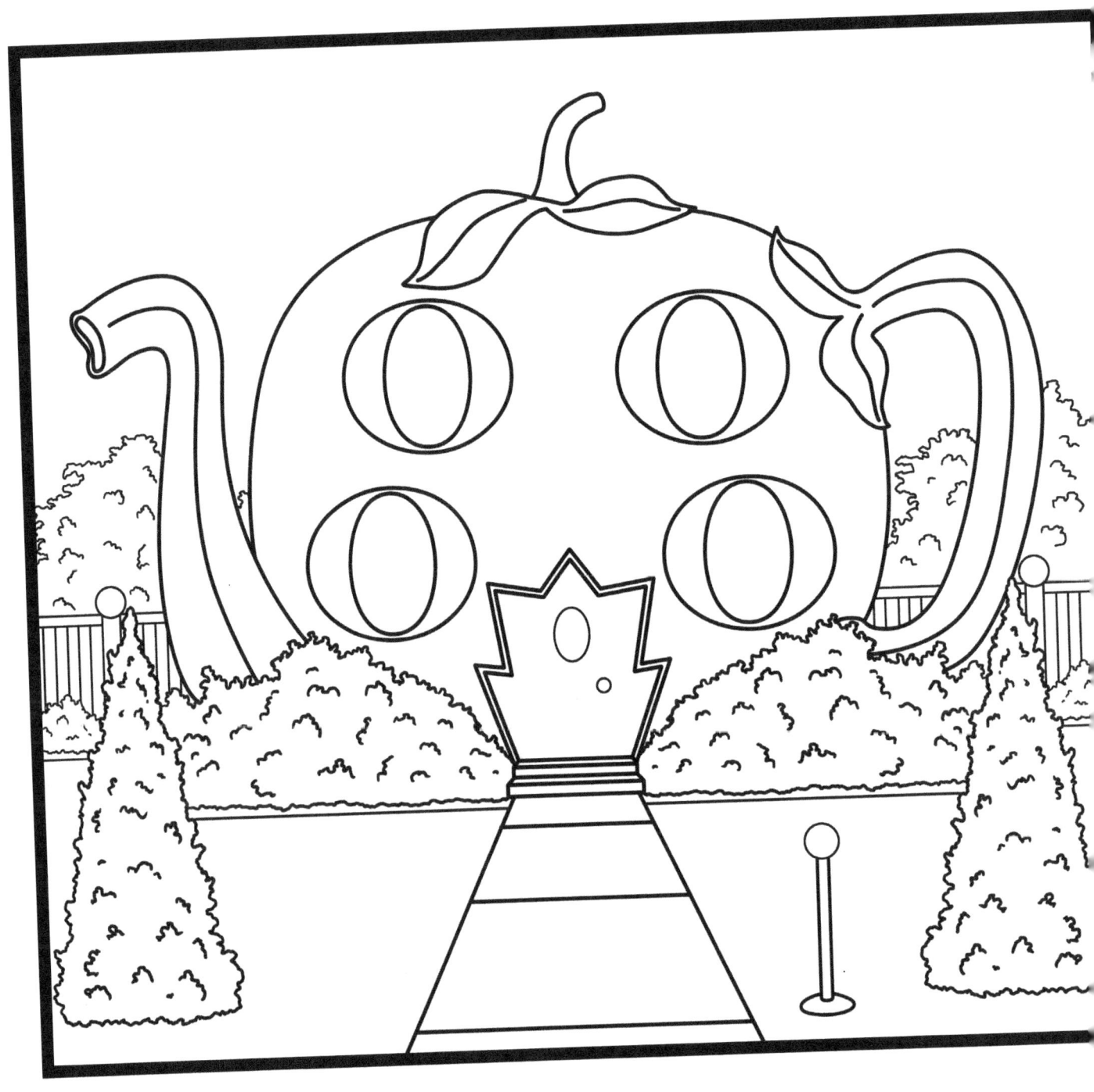

Baby Bus Tea Kettle

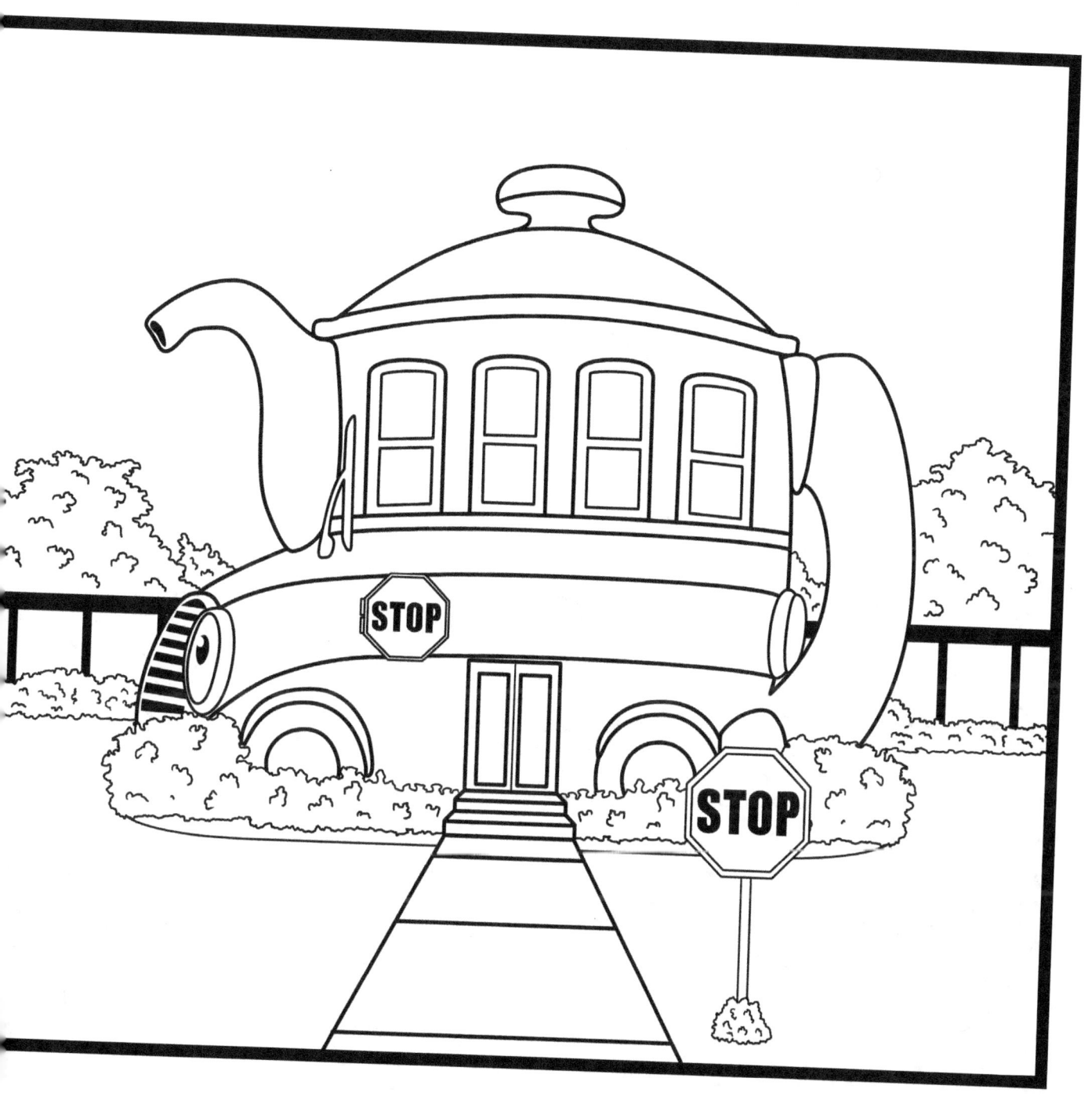

Dominique Thrift Shop

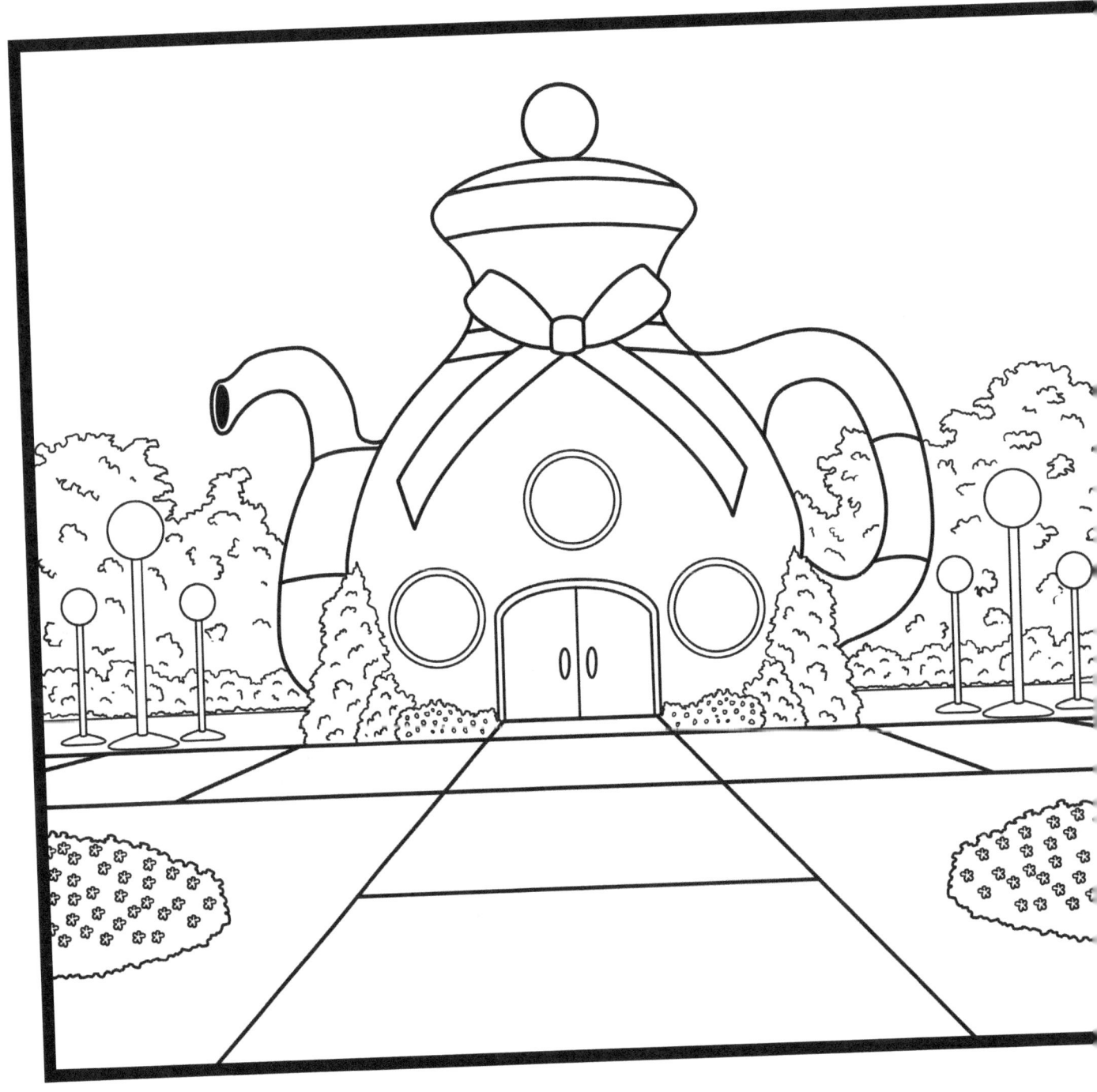

Cherokee House Tea Kettle

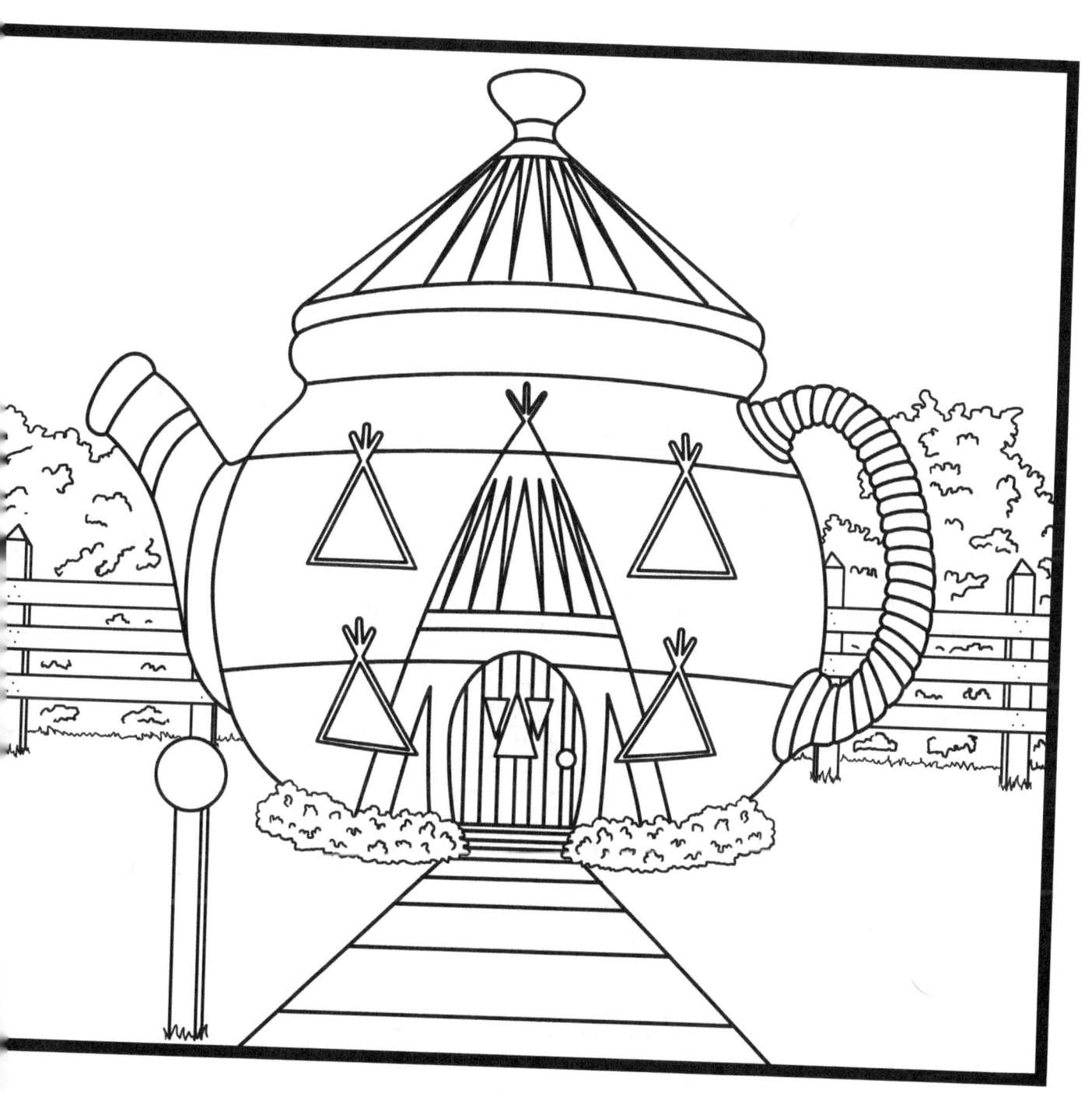

Sue Ling House Tea Kettle

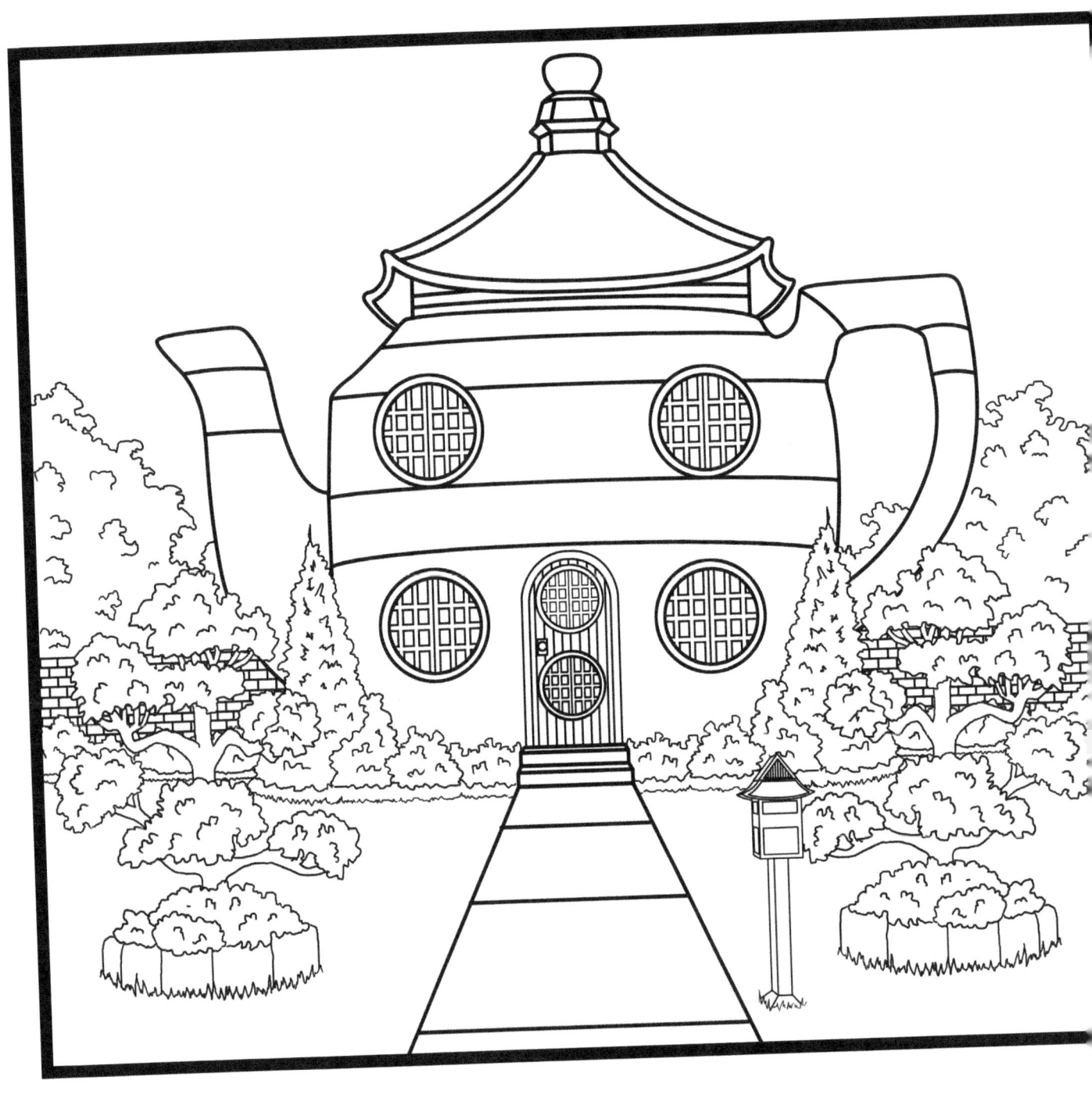

Tennis Dennis Tea Kettle

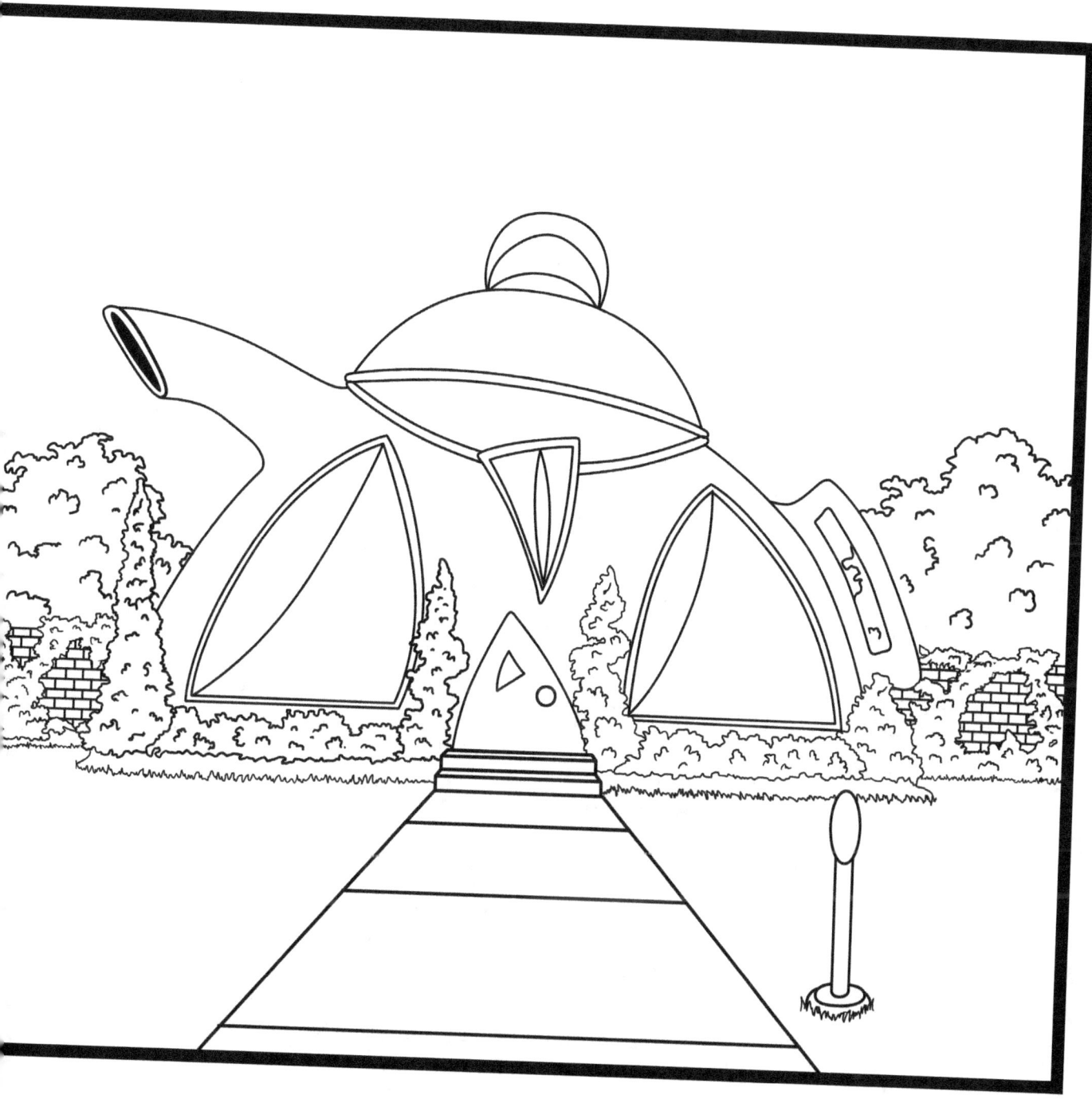

Say Hey Kid Tea Kettle

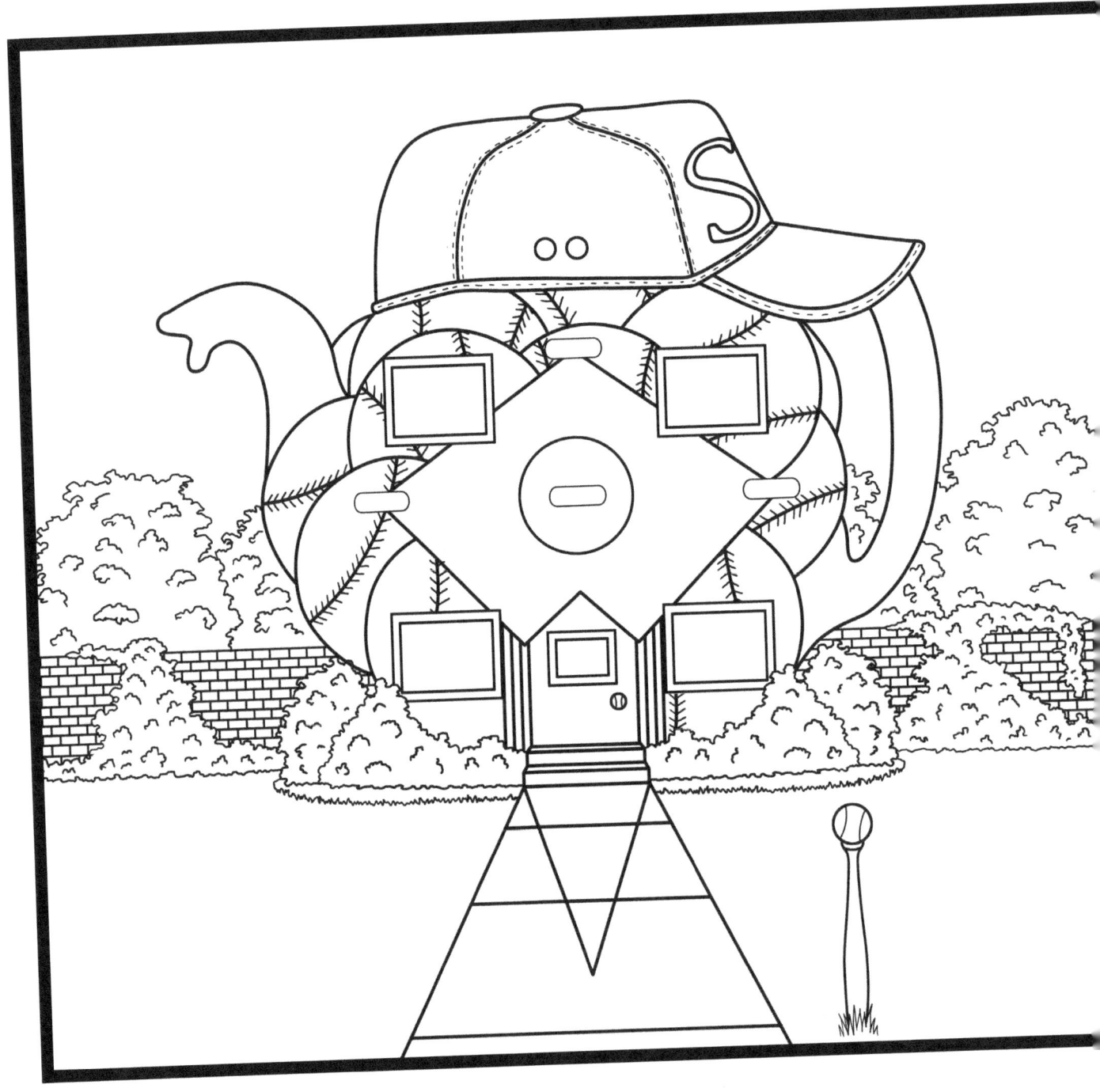

Alicia Delocicioso Tea Kettle

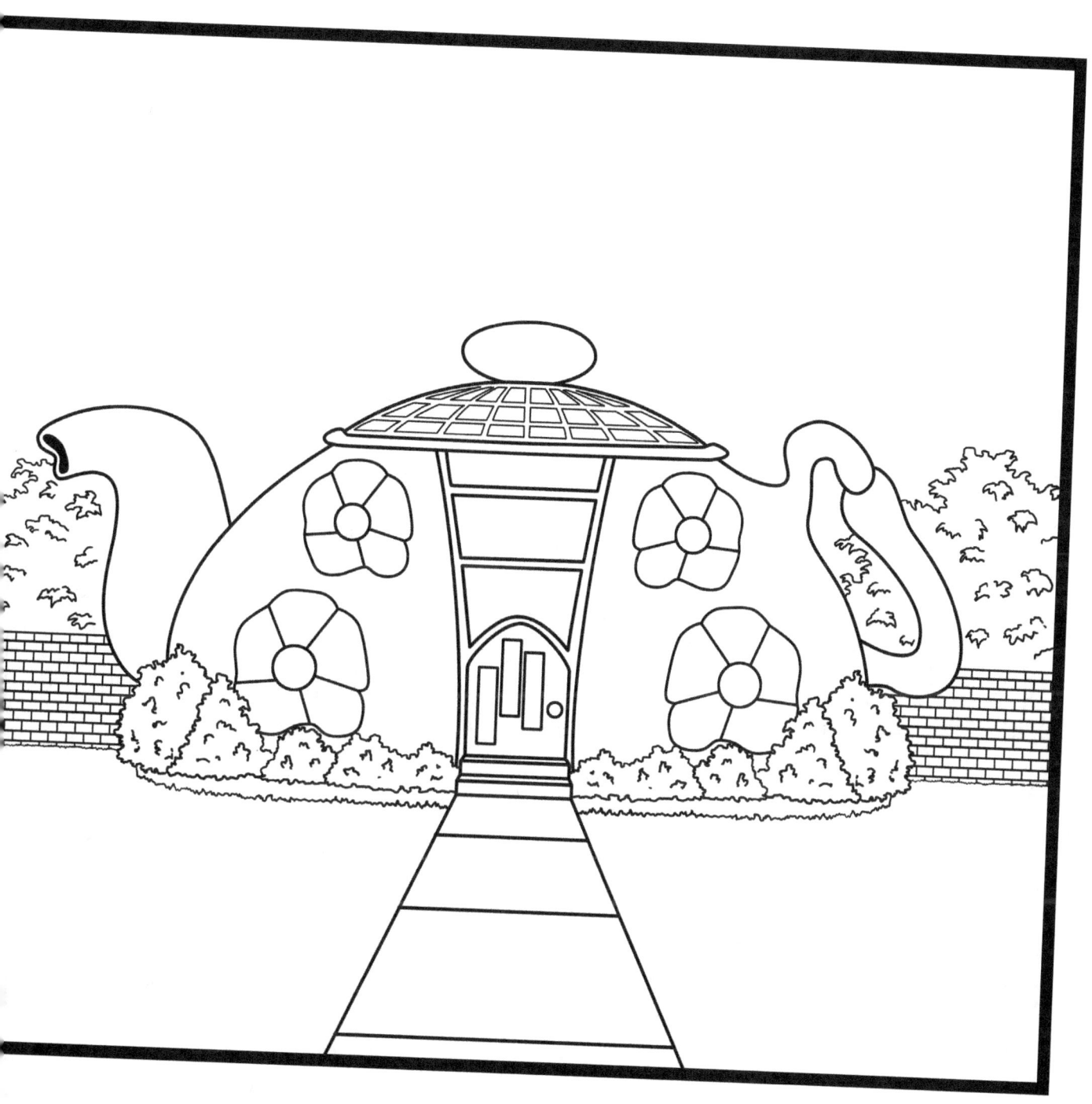

Snicker Doodles Tea Kettle

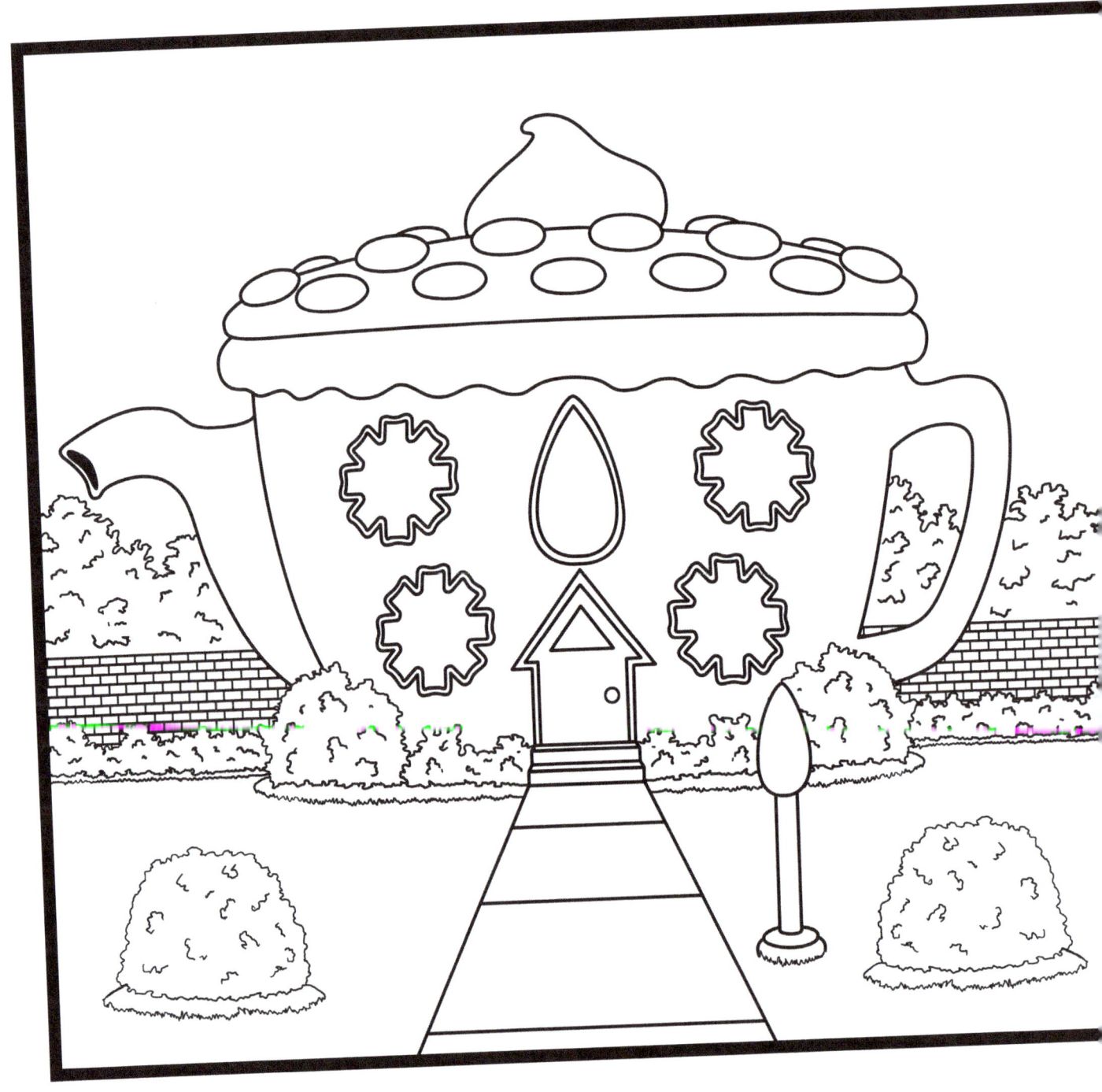

Day Care Tea Kettle

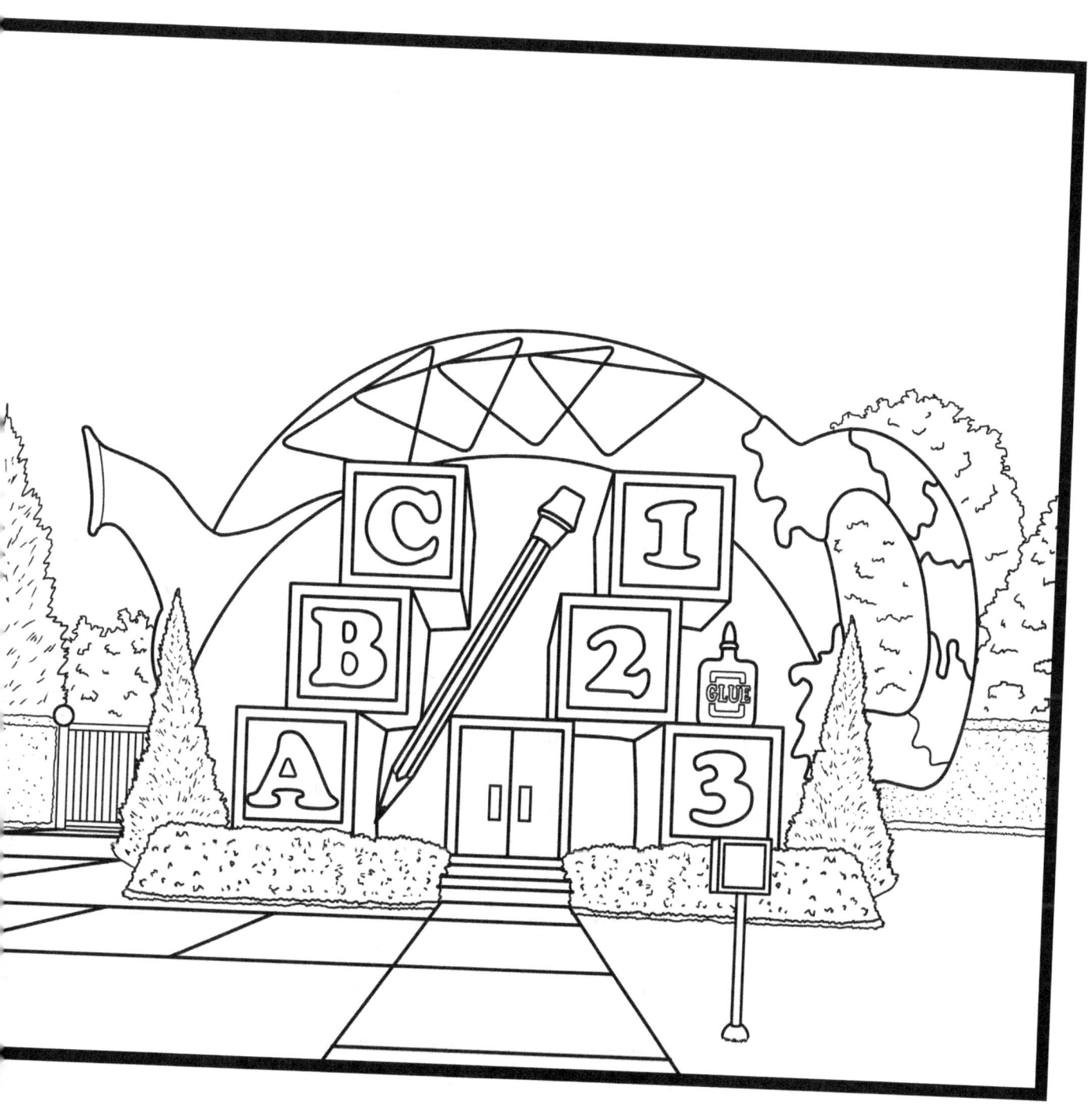

Apple Tart Tea Kettle

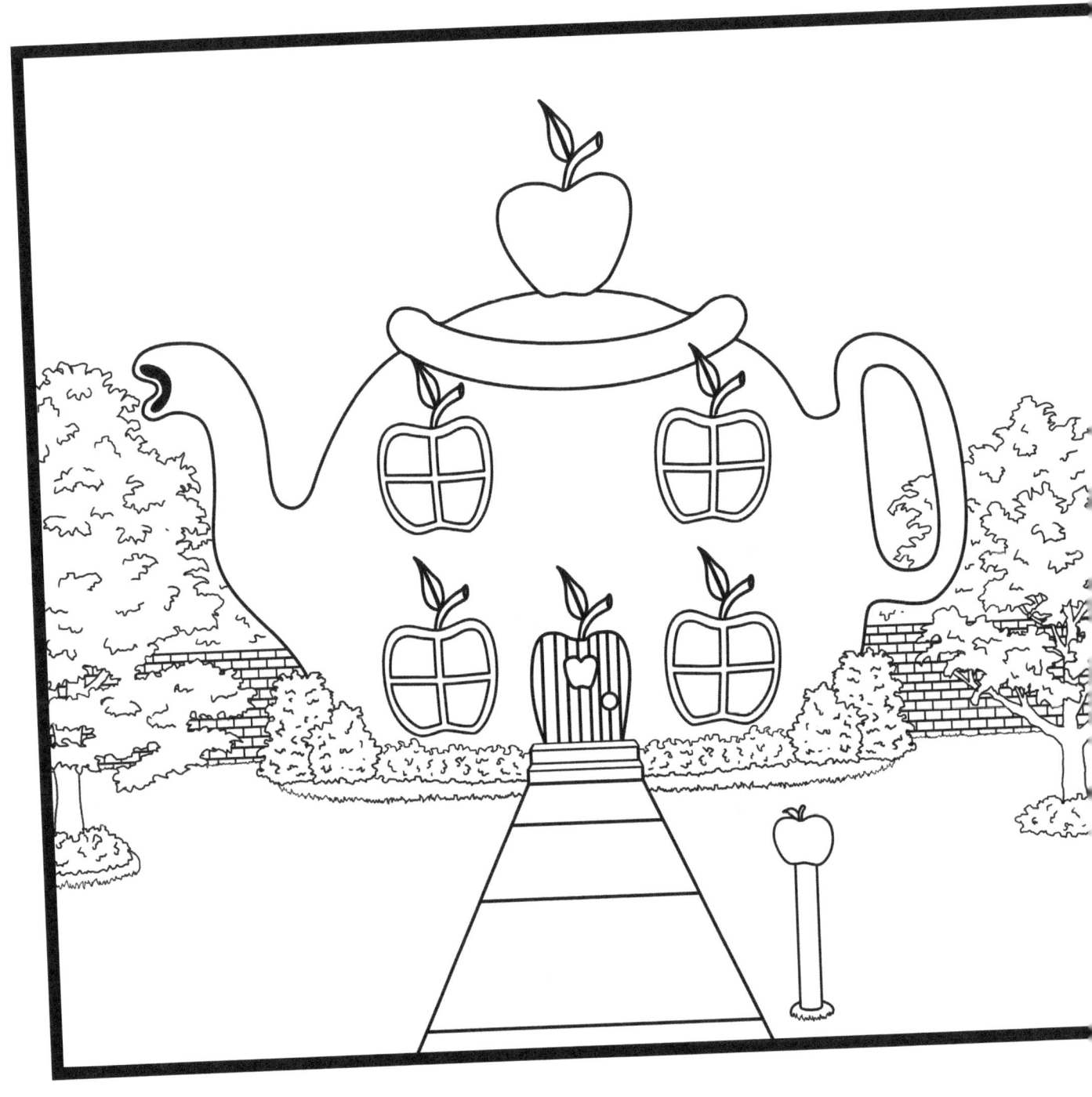

16

Tiana's Flower Patch Tea Kettle

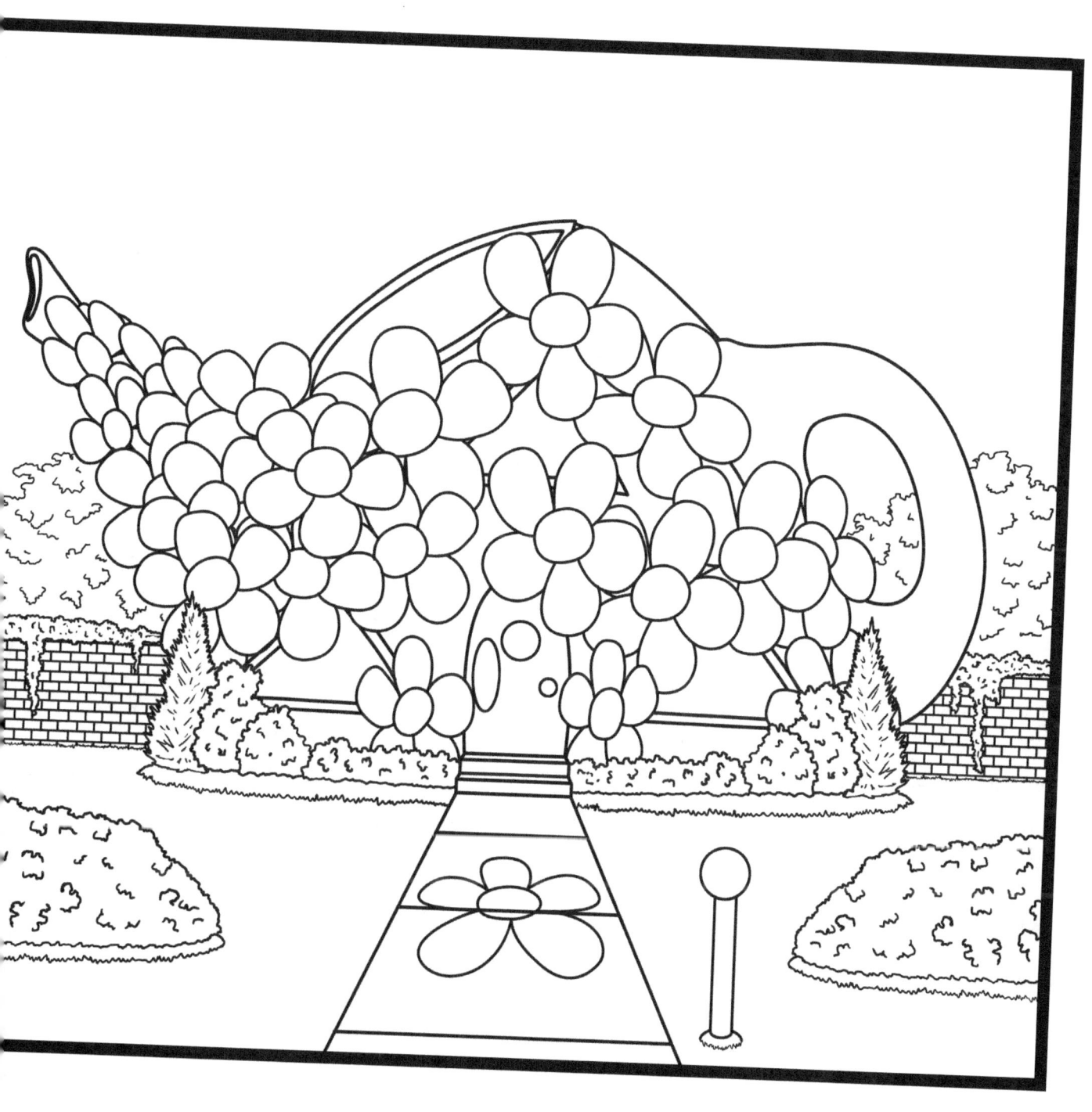

Art Museum Tea Kettle

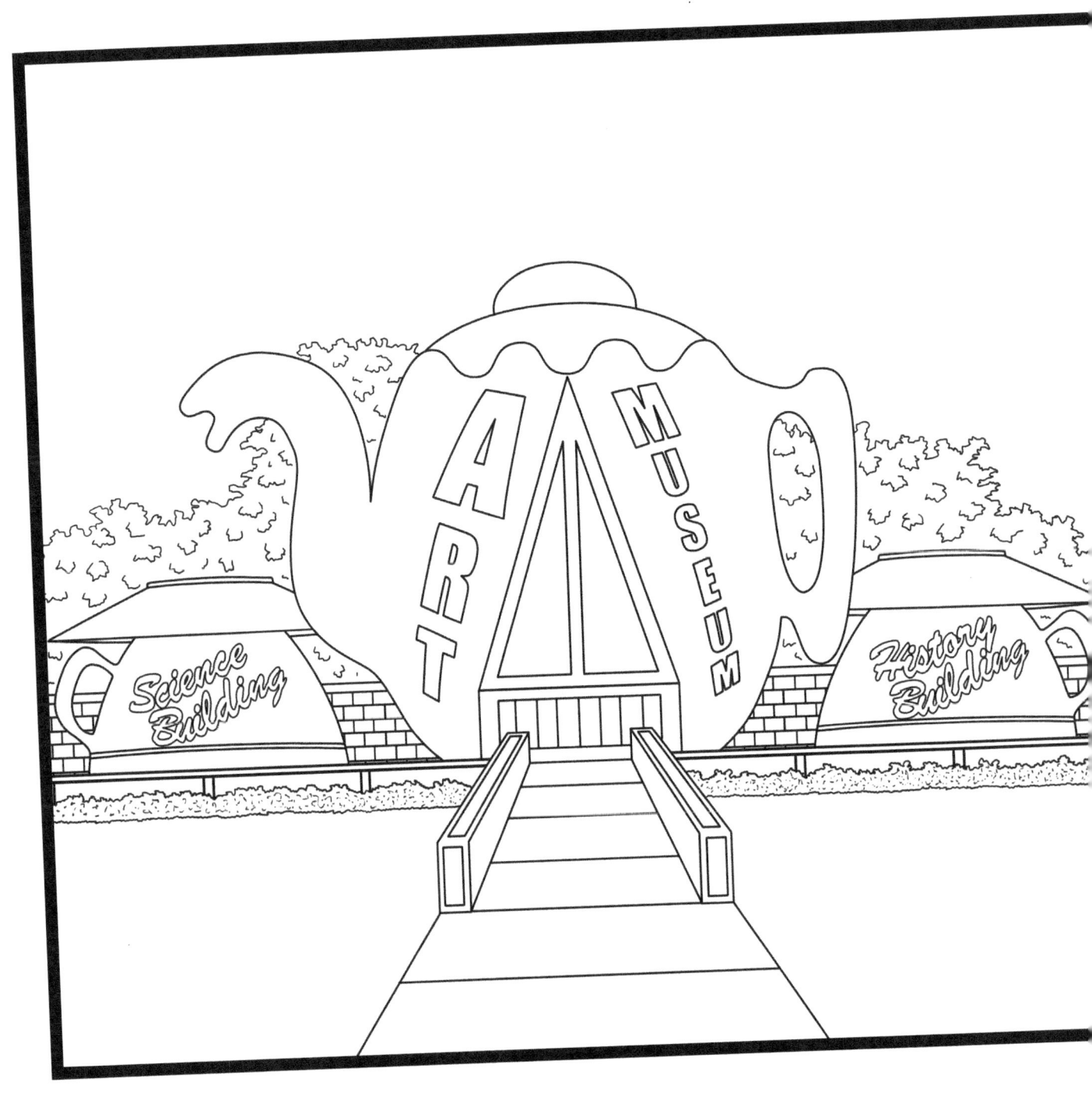

Noble Traits Theater Tea Kettle

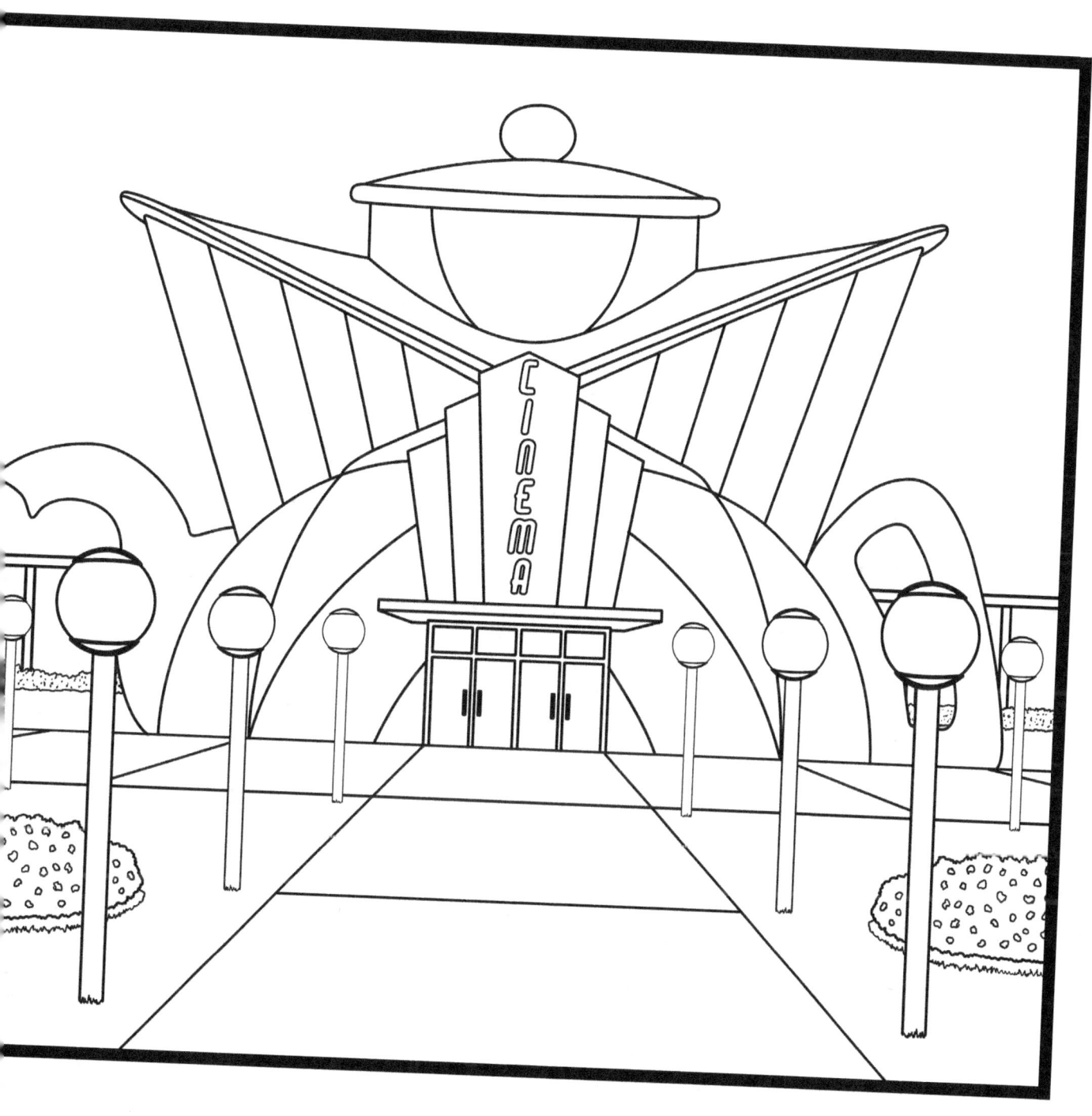

Patty Cakes Tea Kettle

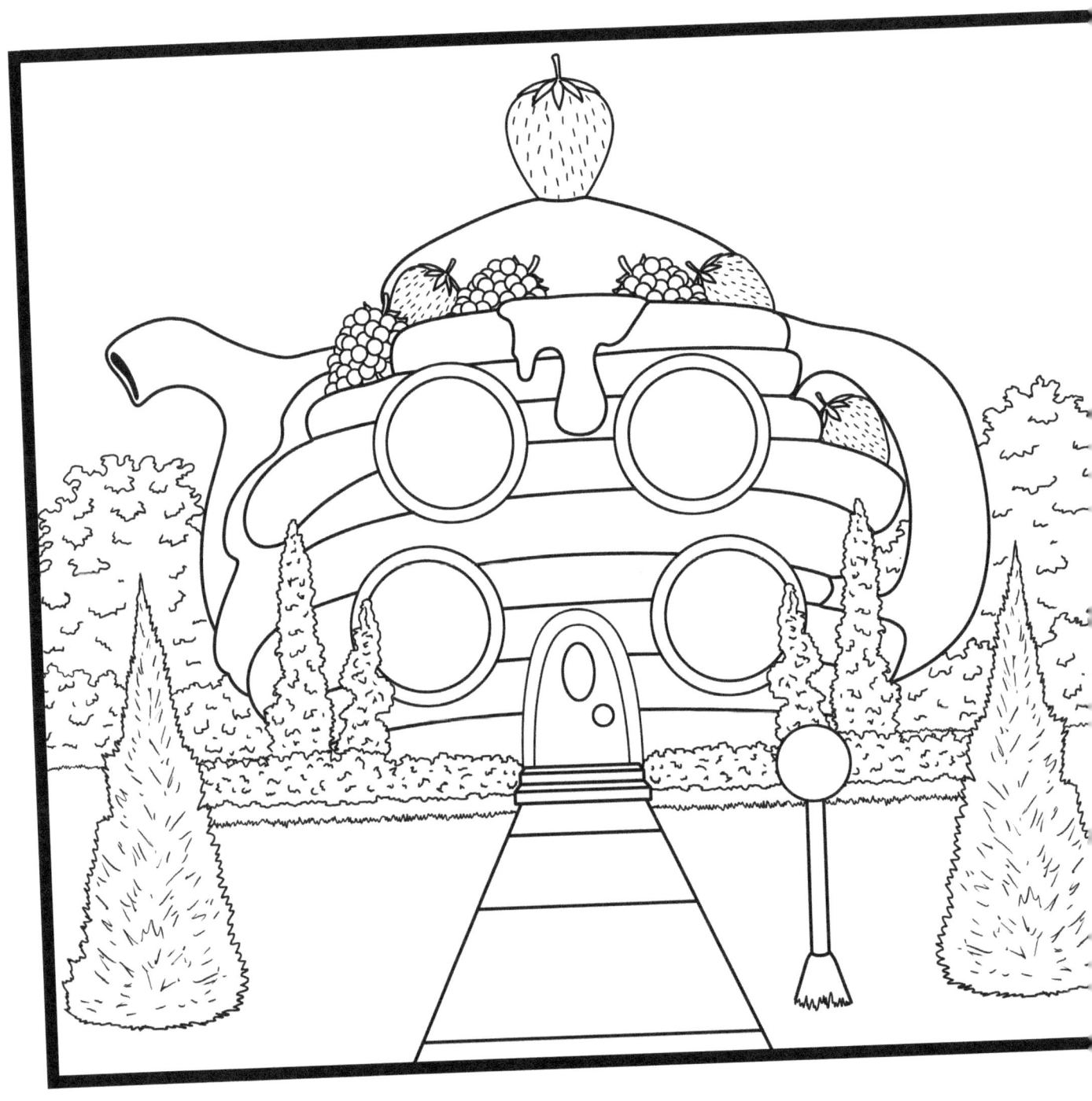

Chocolate Chip Tea Kettle

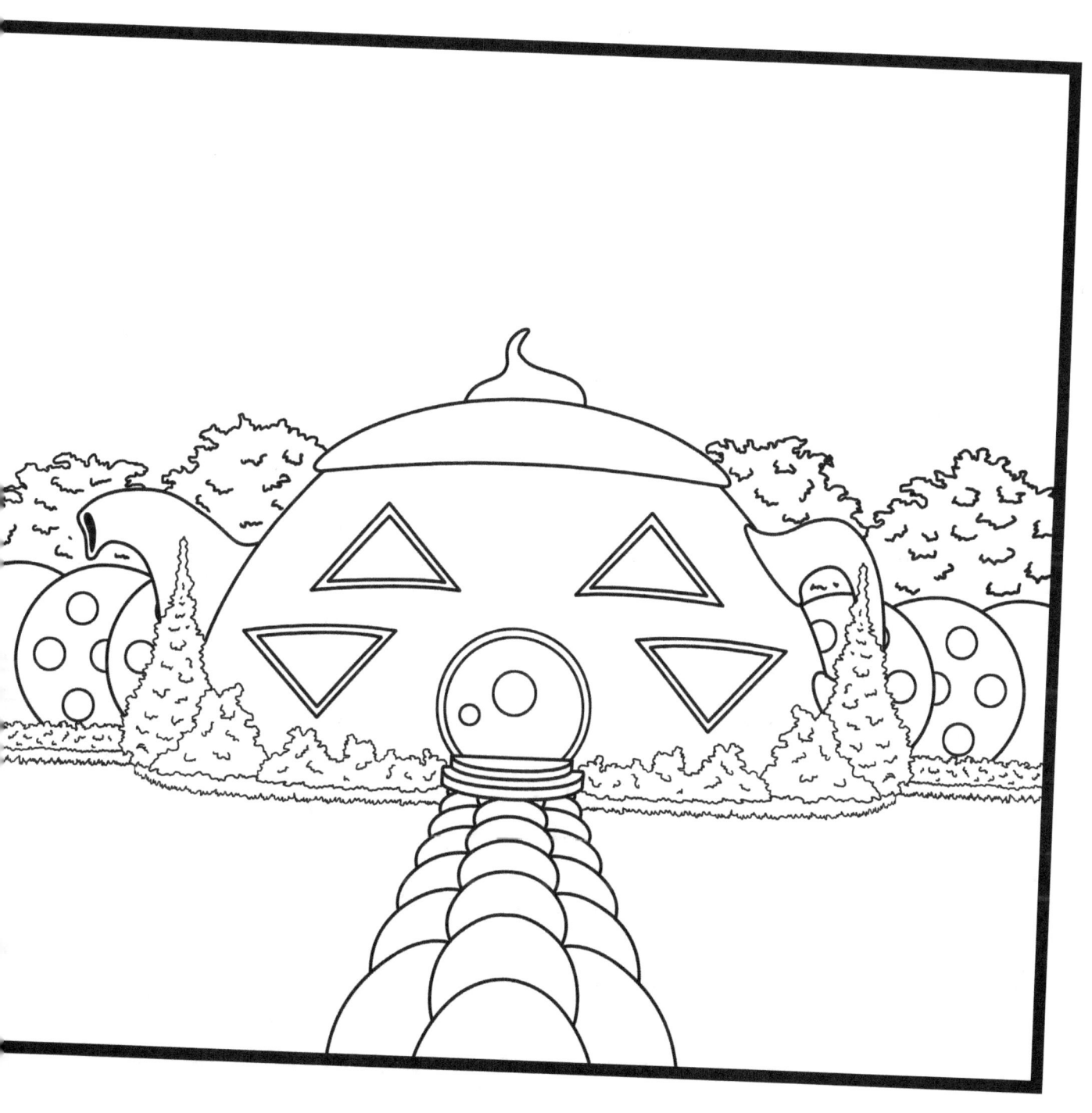

Icy Cups Tea Kettle

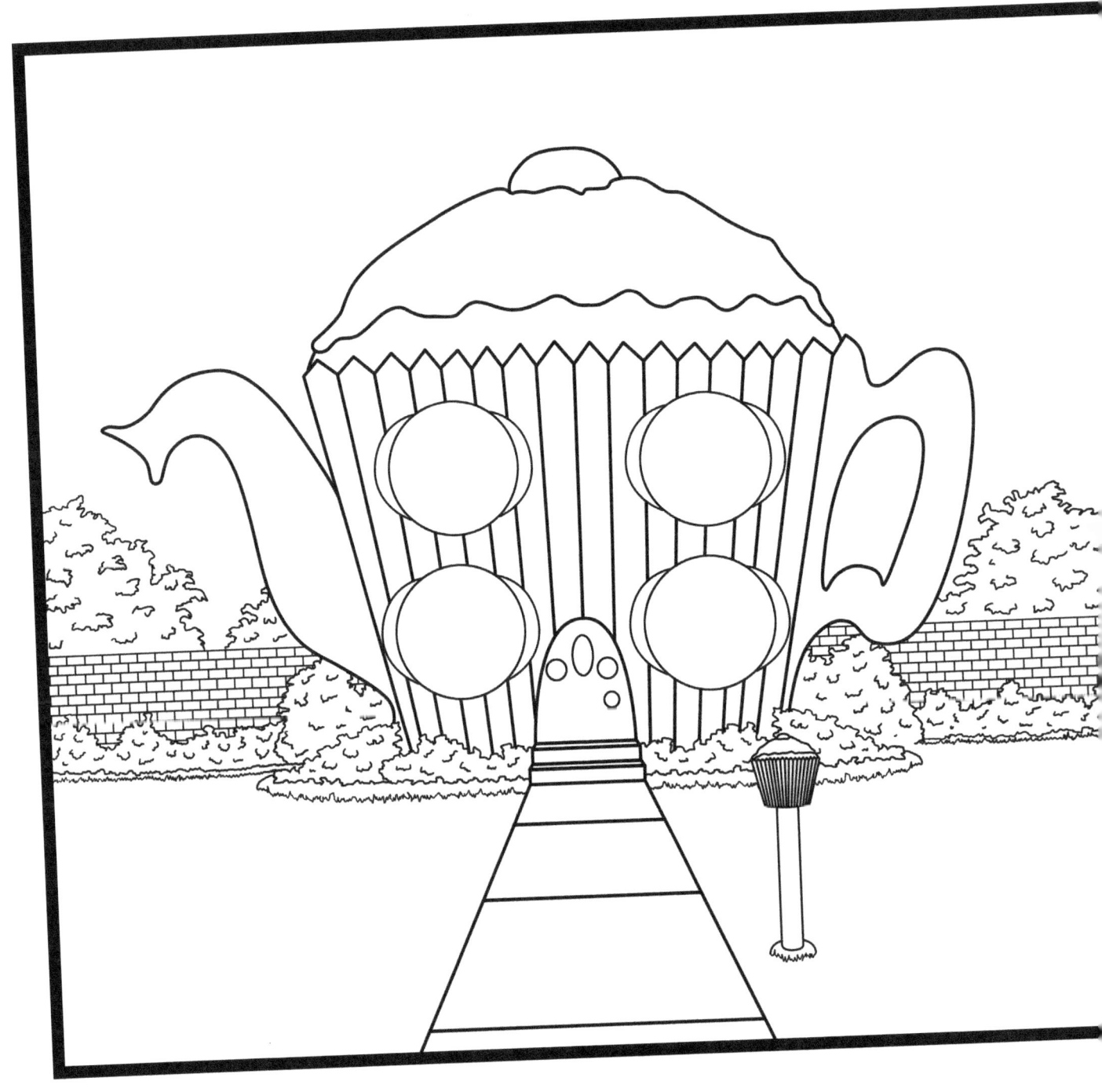

Dezzaraes Thrift Shop Tea Kettle

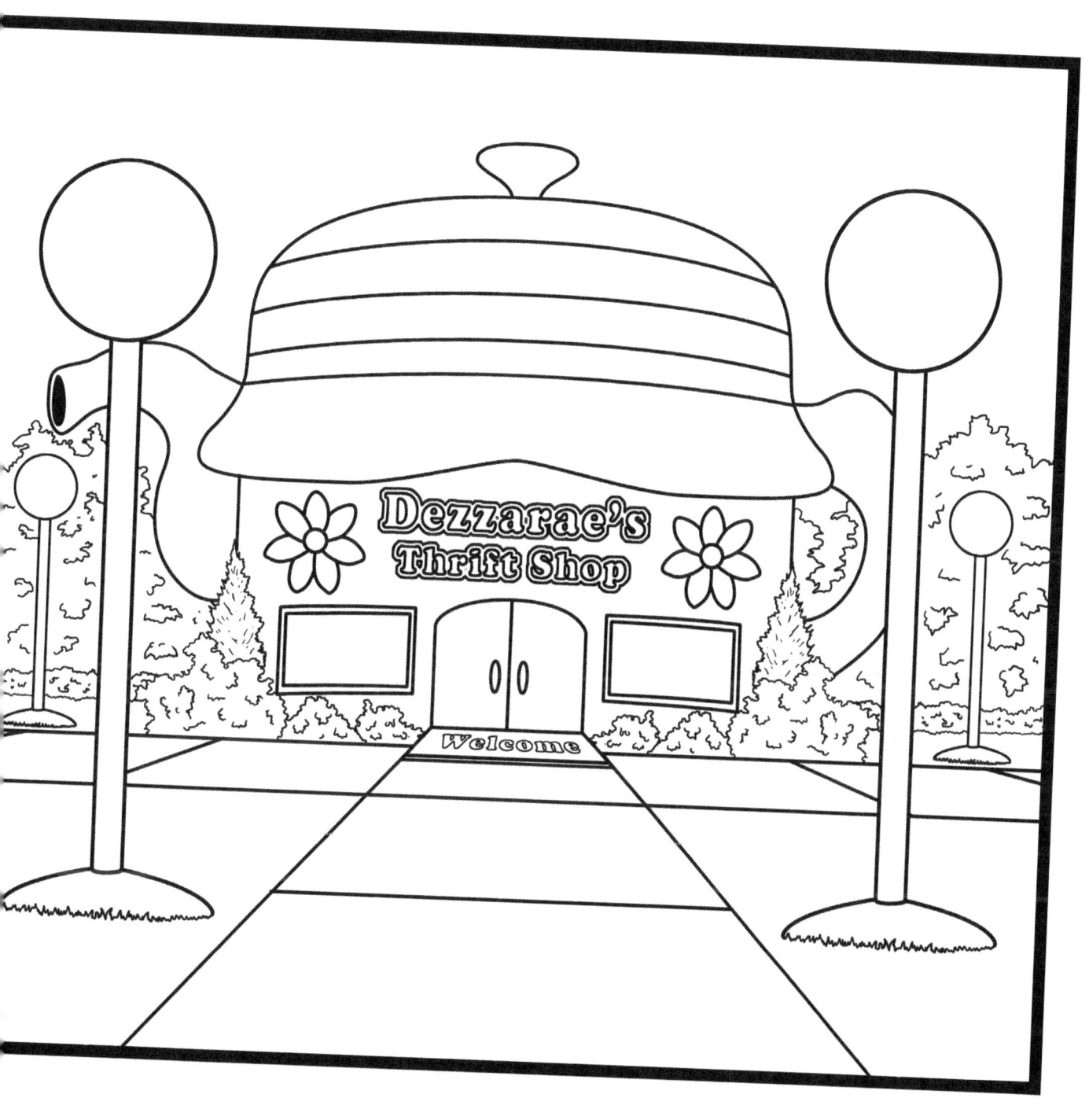

Teahouse Tea Kettle

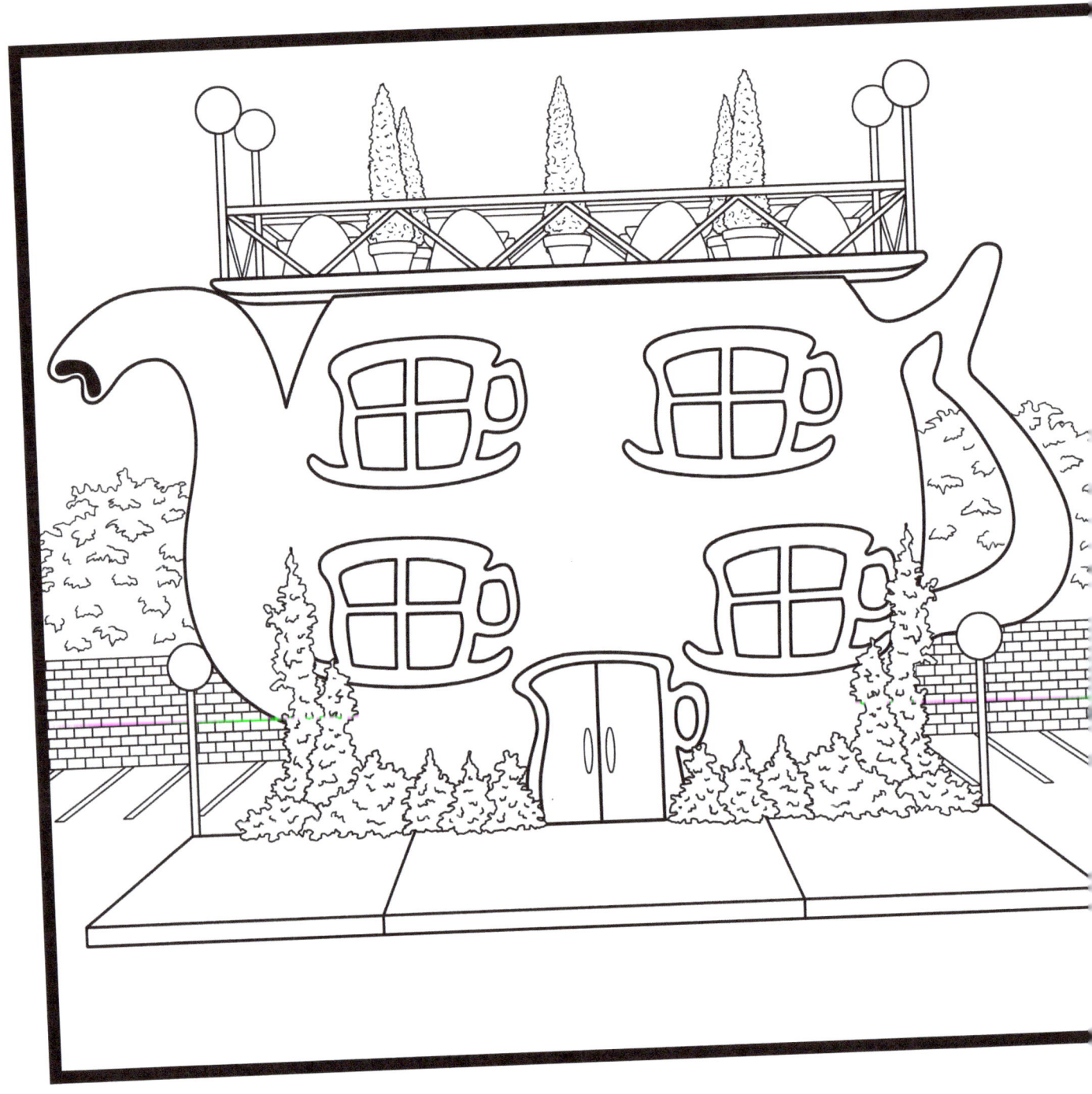

www.ingramcontent.com/pod-product-compliance
Lightning Source LLC
Chambersburg PA
CBHW062210220526
45470CB00009B/2993